Motivation:

The Ultimate Pathway to Motivation and Success like a US NAVY SEAL

John Collins

© Copyright 2015 by John Collins - All rights reserved.

This document is geared towards providing exact and reliable information in regards to the topic and issue covered. The publication is sold with the idea that the publisher is not required to render accounting, officially permitted, or otherwise, qualified services. If advice is necessary, legal or professional, a practised individual in the profession should be ordered.

- From a Declaration of Principles which was accepted and approved equally by a Committee of the American Bar Association and a Committee of Publishers and Associations.

In no way is it legal to reproduce, duplicate, or transmit any part of this document in either electronic means or in printed format. Recording of this publication is strictly prohibited and any storage of this document is not allowed unless with written permission from the publisher. All rights reserved.

The information provided herein is stated to be truthful and consistent, in that any liability, in terms of inattention or otherwise, by any usage or abuse of any policies, processes, or directions contained within is the solitary and utter responsibility of the recipient reader. Under no circumstances will any legal responsibility or blame be held against the publisher for any reparation, damages, or monetary loss due to the information herein, either directly or indirectly.

Respective authors own all copyrights not held by the publisher.

The information herein is offered for informational purposes solely, and is universal as so. The presentation of the information is without contract or any type of guarantee assurance.

The trademarks that are used are without any consent, and the publication of the trademark is without permission or backing by the trademark owner. All trademarks and brands within this book are for clarifying purposes only and are the owned by the owners themselves, not affiliated with this document.

Contents

Introduction 1

Chapter 1: Develop Self-Discipline Like a SEAL 5

Chapter 2: Destroy The Enemy Within – FEAR 9

Chapter 3: Motivation Is All About Mental Models 13

Chapter 4: Replace Lazy Habits with Warrior Habits 19

Chapter 5: Set Goals Like a Courageous Warrior 25

Chapter 6: Hone In On The Target 29

Chapter 7: Train Like an Elite Warrior 33

Chapter 8: Meditate Like a SEAL 39

Conclusion 43

The SEAL Code 45

INTRODUCTION

"It Pays To Be a Winner"

The meaning behind this mantra is that if you refuse to quit and put out as hard as you can for a short period of time, you'll get to rest while everyone else pays for not working as hard. US Navy SEALs are some of the most dangerous men on the planet for this very reason. They learn very early that giving 100% means getting 100%. Hitting the target is ultimately what defines the achievement from the failure.

Giving 95% usually gives a return of 60% and giving 90% will get you a 40% return.

Think about it. Where does this show up in your life? When have you received the maximum benefit in your life? It was while you were playing all out and were giving it 100%!

Life is about going the extra mile. That is what makes the difference between success and failure.

Success in the battlefield and in life is also about being prepared and acting decisively in the moment. Going on the battlefront is not easy, you come up against terrorists, enemies, spies and all sorts of deadly people who challenge your very existence. As a result you have to be decisive. You must be ready to make up your mind quickly, conscious of the fact that your decision will affect the lives of many. You will need a sharp mind and sound body.

SEALS spend years preparing for some of the most dangerous moments imaginable. A large part of this work is done mentally by pushing the limits of their minds. The path to success begins with winning the war within. Get comfortable being uncomfortable.

> **"Seals don't quit when they're tired they quit when they're done."**

If your solution to being tired is quitting, then you are everything that is wrong in our world. For US Navy Seals quitting is only done at completion. Perseverance is the key to overcoming adversity. Success comes one small step at a time, so never quit!

For SEALs, the ongoing goal is to achieve excellence. This becomes a lifelong habit for them long after they complete being in service. Set your goals high and never lower your personal and professional standard.

Attitude is contagious – Be a positive force in all the things you do and stay away from those who doubt you. 60% of people don't care about your problems and the other 40% are glad you have them.

You must plan your life around being fully functional all the time. You need to be on the move, you have to be a doer, not one of those chaps whose emphasis in life is all about theory and ideas. You need to be moving, doing, and finishing at all times. Ideas are great, but action is what gets it done. SEALs are always doing something.

How do SEALs get motivation? Motivation comes from within, they internalize it by reconnecting with their purpose. They call this "the gut check". Never allow anyone to tell you that you cannot achieve something.

Motivation can be defined as the reason that an individual has to do something, to behave or act in a given manner. It can also be a theoretical construct often used to understand behavior, the willingness or general desire of an individual to do something.

Whatever inspires you to be who you are, do what you do, and strive to become a better individual, you must make sure that you commit and follow it daily.

CHAPTER 1: DEVELOP SELF-DISCIPLINE LIKE A SEAL

Everything that you want to achieve in this life is possible, especially if you have the self-discipline to help you go the extra mile. There are a lot of things that you would perhaps want to achieve, but as long as you do not have that self-drive to push forward like a Navy Seal, you will struggle to achieve these targets.

So, what does it take to get there? What do you need to give you the push you need to get over the line?

Self-discipline

Self-discipline is something that a lot of us struggle with. Most people want to be supervised all the time for them to do what they were supposed to be doing in the first place. If you are such a person, you are already making all the wrong moves.

Self-discipline is the ability to make yourself do what you should do when you should do it whether you feel like it or not.

Get out of Bed

Some would say that the early hours of the morning are the most productive hours. They say that more can be accomplished during this time than during the rest of their day.

In basic SEAL training, SEALs begin their day at 5am. You have no business sleeping in if you want to win in life. Get in the habit of getting up earlier and get more done.

Make the bed

Making your bed is the best possible way to begin your day. If you make your bed every morning you will have accomplished the first task of the day. It will give you a small sense of pride and it will encourage you to do another task and another and another. By the end of the day that one small task will have turned into many tasks completed. Making your bed also reinforces the fact that little things in life do matter. If you can't do the little things right, you'll never learn to do the big things right.

Use a reward system

In Basic SEAL training, SEAL's that win are rewarded by having hot meals indoors while wearing dry clothes. If they fail to achieve their intended goal then it's a half mile run down the beach to roll around in the cold ocean followed by eating a cold meal outside in wet clothes. Hence the saying "It pays to be a winner"

You do not necessarily need to make your life as hard as the Navy Seals do, but if it gets you positive results then why not? You should come up with a reward system, where you reward yourself for meeting your goals.

Don't QUIT Ever!

You must have heard the phrase "winners never quit and quitters never win". There is no room for quitting. As long as you have a plan to work on, you must make sure that you follow through with it to the end. There are more people who would rather watch you fail than watch you succeed. Don't give them the satisfaction. SEALs say, "If your brain says you're done, you're only 40% done." Keep going.

Wait it Out

There is nothing more important to a Navy Seal than understanding the virtue of patience. Self-Discipline like a SEAL requires immense patience. A SEAL sniper can wait on a target for days if necessary. Calm yourself down and wait out the traffic jam you are in. No one can trust someone who indulges in their emotions. Staying calm will give you the ability to read and understand the situation before you make your move. This is a very good way of preventing wrong decisions that we often regret later.

Disciplined

Once you have figured out the plan that you want to work on, the next course of action will be for you to adhere to it. Many people fail to do this. There are many plans that start well and before long they get tossed out of the window.

Getting up at 5am so you can hit the gym before work sucks! Being fat and out of shape sucks a lot more! Not hitting the snooze button takes discipline. Navy SEALs are disciplined.

Find a mentor or life coach

No ultra-successful person ever got to where they are on their own. A mentor or a life coach is someone who will make sure that you stay focused. This is someone who will ensure that you barely ever go out of line. This is someone who is not afraid to tell you the truth and to hold you accountable to your commitments.

You also want someone who will inspire you to greatness. Motivation and success are like any other project that you may take on. It's imperative to find an expert in this arena, someone who has already charted this area and is willing to be your guide.

Chapter 2: Destroy The Enemy Within - FEAR

FEAR – The one thing that keeps us all away from our dreams and ambitions. The funny thing about fear, it is all in your head. Until the day you conquer it and defeat it like the enemy it is, you will never be able to get from one point to the other.

A careful analysis at how fear prevents us from achieving our dreams and goals will show you that in real sense, it is not even fear that hinders you from being the best you can ever be, it is you. Every other time we hide our own inhibitions in the name of fear, when in the real sense, the biggest problem, the enemy within, is ourselves.

Once you are able to get fear out of its comfort zone in your life, you will be able to push through and overcome all obstacles.

Define your biggest obstacles and push through

There is no better way to push through discomfort to the point where you are able to reach your goals, than to inspire yourself to overcome the challenges. Some people look towards others to inspire them to greatness, while others simply inspire themselves.

There is no one better than yourself to do this. You know what you want to achieve in life, so you also know when you are falling short of these expectations. This should therefore make it easier for you to strive to become better.

The disappointments that you face today are not supposed to dampen your spirit, or overshadow your dreams for tomorrow. They are supposed to make you realize just how determined you are to overcome.

The following are 4 important things that will help you do this:

- Determine the potential challenges that you face in life, and set your mind on meeting them.
- Take a keen notice on your emotions, and do not resist them either.
- Challenge yourself, challenge your emotions to become a better person.
- Do not ignore the minor victories; celebrate them. It is upon their foundation that you will build on for greater victories that lie ahead.

Widen your capacity for action

One of the biggest challenges that we face when we harbor fear in our lives, is to minimize the scope of what we can do, in the process only succeeding at limiting our ability to shine. Everyone has a purpose in this life. The only way you can achieve your purpose is to work hard to beat the odds.

Turning obstacles into opportunities will help you become more accomplished in life. You will change the way you see life, your view of obstacles will never be the same, and before you know it, your view of life will be different too.

Once again, we have to stress the importance of small victories. You will be lying to yourself if you set out to achieve a mammoth task all at once, though it would not hurt to try. The problem with going all out, is the risk of the repercussions when you fail. This is the reason why it is advisable to realize that you can make it, and work out a plan to achieve this one step at a time.

Widening your capacity for action calls for a deeper understanding of yourself as a person. There are things that we take for granted in life, which actually do count for so much in the long run.

Think about exercise for example, some of us barely give it a few minutes of our day, not until we realize we are overweight and none of our clothes fit us. That's when we start rushing into every other diet program that we can come across, looking for miracles.

Remember that at times, even the types of people you surround yourself with, will determine the outcome of this venture.

Stop Bullshitting yourself – Be open to criticism and take value from it

No one is perfect, that's the mere precept of life. We are all on a journey, one wherein we are supposed to become better versions tomorrow, of the person we are today. Criticism is not a bad thing. As a matter of fact, people will only criticize you because they have recognized your presence, or something that you have done.

If you go through life without being criticized, you need to change the environment where you live, because it is not healthy. There might be a lot of things you are doing so wrong, but no one has the guts to tell it to your face.

You are not only supposed to be open to criticism, but you must get some value from it, learn from it. But how should you do this?

- Learn to stop your first reaction to the criticism.

- The most important thing about criticism is to turn the negatives into what do I need to learn here?
- Never forget to appreciate the critic, thank them for being brutally honest
- Strive to become better today than you were yesterday

Let all challenges be a game

There is nothing better than winning a game. It fills you with such enthusiasm and you yearn to keep winning. This is what you need to do with your challenges. Once you have them all mapped out, imagine them being a game, where your only struggle is to be better and win every other time.

Say for example, your current challenge in life is to create wealth. This will be your new game, Wealth Creation. You will have small plans outlined where you will be able to make small winnings from time to time, with your eyes on the bigger prize.

Every win in the game, is a win over your challenges. Better yet every win, is a win for you, as you will be able to empower yourself to be better.

Parting shot!

There is nothing like fear. Fear is just an idea that you have in your mind. It is a concept that you have created, and keeps holding you back, pushes you into a comfort zone, and prevents you from achieving your true potential.

Overcome fear, and you will unlock your life to greater things.

Chapter 3: Motivation Is All About Mental Models

SEALs win every mission before they ever attack. They see victory before ever beginning the mission. They visualize success at an individual level and at a team level. This is called winning in the mind. The power of visualization cements victory by attracting the power of positive and clear thinking.

This is one of many principles of winning that US Navy SEALs use, and it starts in the mind. You have to craft your destiny. Use your own mind to build the future that you desire.

Elimination of self-doubt

"Do today what others won't. Do tomorrow what others can't."

We need to take ourselves to a challenge. We grow from challenge. If we avoid challenge we stunt our growth. It is only human for you to get to a point where you doubt your abilities to succeed, you doubt your ability to overcome the challenges ahead of you. As we all know for sure, there are challenges that present us with unimaginable options. There are challenges that make you feel like whichever option you choose, you are still going to remain doomed.

It is during these times that the feeling of self-doubt checks into the presidential suite in your mind. Woe unto you if you allow it to settle in. Doubt, like fear, is but a concept. You can never know how far you can go without making the effort. It is close to impossible for you to even consider making any progress in life if you constantly doubt your abilities.

There are so many people who are afraid of falling, however, how can you fall if you do not wish to climb higher? If you keep shying away from opportunities, there will never be an opportune time for you. Over time you will be overtaken even by those who were less ambitious than you are right now.

Respond to challenges

How do you normally respond to challenging situations in life? Are you the type that hides away into a corner and comes out when the coast is clear, or do you face your fears head on? Challenges are supposed to make you grow, they help you become a better individual over time.

In as much as challenges will in most cases appear to be difficult, you must understand that constantly avoiding them will only keep stunting your growth process.

Motivational information can also make you go so far. Think about reading motivational books in your free time, listening to motivational talks and speeches, music and so forth. Individuals like Jack Canfield and Tony Robbins are great at cracking us open and inspiring us in our lives and our choices.

SEAL Affirmations

The Navy Seals are no joke. With so many individuals volunteering to be a part of the selection process, it takes more than just hard work to make it. Each and every day is more than just a challenge, the participants are pushed further, tested to their limits, to the point where they go as far as possible as mental annihilation is concerned.

The trainers purposely push the applicants to quit in order to separate the strong from the weak. There can be no weak SEALs. There is a bell in the center of all the barracks which is used to signify a SEAL candidate quitting and going home. They simply ring the bell and all the discomfort and stress is over.

The selection process alone, sees more than 80% of the candidates dropping out. However, let's focus on the close to 20% who do graduate. What makes them different? What makes them think any different than the rest of us? The secret lies in the motivational mantras that they live by. The following are some of these special quotes:

There are two ways of doing something...The right way, and Again!
- If something is worth all your time and energy, it certainly is worth doing over and over until you get it right.

It's all mind over matter, If I don't mind, then it doesn't matter – If you have to go against the grain to achieve success, then nothing else matters; go against the grain

On your backs, on your bellies, on your backs, on your bellies.....feet! – Change happens when you least expect it, but you have to respond appropriately

You don't have to like it, you just have to do it – There are situations in life where you will simply need to grit your teeth and hit the ground running.

Training to be a Navy SEAL is painful, but as you get stronger, you do not feel as much pain
The only easy day was Yesterday!

Create a vision board

Visualization is one of the most powerful mind exercises you can do. Creating a space or reminder that displays what you want actually does bring it to life. What we focus on expands.

The vision board will act as a daily reminder and thought provoker. Thoughts will be created every time you see the board. It is a proven fact that what we think about the most manifests in our lives.

It's important to include how you want to feel on your vision board as well as the things that you want to attain. Find pictures that represent or symbolize the experiences, feelings and possessions that you want to attract into your life, and place them on your board. Use magazine cutouts, photographs, Navy SEAL mantras and whatever inspires you. Include anything that speaks to you and watch what happens.

Navy SEAL Ethos

"In times of war or uncertainty there is a special breed of warrior ready to answer our Nation's call. A common man with uncommon desire to succeed. Forged by adversity, he stands alongside America's finest special operations forces to serve his country, the American people, and protect their way of life. I am that man.

My Trident is a symbol of honor and heritage. Bestowed upon me by the heroes that have gone before, it embodies the trust of those I have sworn to protect. By wearing the Trident I accept the responsibility of my chosen profession and way of life. It is a privilege that I must earn every day. My loyalty to Country and Team is beyond reproach. I humbly serve as a guardian to my fellow Americans always ready to defend those who are unable to defend themselves. I do not advertise the nature of my work, nor seek recognition for my actions. I voluntarily accept the inherent hazards of my profession, placing the welfare and security of others before my own. I serve with honor on and off the battlefield. The ability to control my emotions and my actions, regardless of circumstance, sets me apart from other men. Uncompromising integrity is my standard. My character and honor are steadfast. My word is my bond.

We expect to lead and be led. In the absence of orders I will take charge, lead my teammates and accomplish the mission. I lead by example in all situations. I will never quit. I persevere and thrive on adversity. My Nation expects me to be physically harder and mentally stronger than my enemies. If knocked down, I will get back up, every time. I will draw on every remaining ounce of strength to protect my teammates and to accomplish our mission. I am never out of the fight.

We demand discipline. We expect innovation. The lives of my teammates and the success of our mission depend on me – my technical skill, tactical proficiency, and attention to detail. My training is never complete. We train for war and fight to win. I stand ready to bring the full spectrum of combat power to bear in order to achieve my mission and the goals established by my country. The execution of my duties will be swift and violent when required yet guided by the very principles that I serve to defend. Brave men have fought and died building the proud tradition and feared reputation that I am bound to uphold. In the worst of conditions, the legacy of my teammates steadies my resolve and silently guides my every deed. I will not fail."

Chapter 4: Replace Lazy Habits with Warrior Habits

Our lives revolve around our habits. Some of these habits have sometimes taken years to form and others can be formed in a matter of hours. As you already know, once you have a created a bad habit it can be a real struggle drop it. Our habits allow us to run on autopilot doing the same things over and over day after day.

We waste a lot of time every other day doing things that do not add value to our lives. It is obvious that you might be tempted to wonder what if you were to eliminate them from your life. Things like watching too much TV, surfing the internet, and playing video games. More than 90% of the things that we do every day are based on habit. Change your habits, change your life. It's that simple.

How to go about it

Just in case you are wondering how you are going to go about this, it is rather easy. It will take a little bit of organization and coordination from your part. Start with planning your day.

Anyone who goes about their day without a plan is definitely destined for failure. Put down a list of the things that you need to do for the day. Prioritize them, with the challenging ones coming earlier in the day when you are still fresh.

Select one of the goals, draw a mark on it so that it is conspicuous, and make sure that you work on it and complete it before the day is over.

Having your life going according to book might sound like taking you back to your school days when teachers were strict, but you must also remember that if you are after success like a Navy Seal, the only easy day was yesterday!

- Become goal oriented

Develop the habit of setting realistic and unrealistic goals. One of the most unrealistic goals a SEAL candidate will set is the completion of Hell Week. You don't sleep for a week. You run countless miles with heavy backpacks. You swim in the frigid ocean for dozens of miles. All of this is done while battling second stage hypothermia, sores and often minor fractures. Imagine the confidence one feels after achieving this goal. Unrealistic goals get us closer than we ever would have imagined.

- Become results oriented

Results are your metrics. How do you know how much further you need to go? How do you know where you need to put in more work for next time? You need results. Did I increase my monthly income goal of 10K per month? Yes / No. Your results must be specific and measureable.

- Become People oriented

True success in battle is about relationships. It's about trust, honor and the man next to you. Every SEAL knows 100% that the man next to him will be able to save his life. Take care of others and you will always be taken care of yourself.

- Become health oriented

You must be conscious about your health if you are to become any better in this venture. You already worked out a diet that you want to keep. You have already thought of the foods that you need to eliminate or ration from your meals.

- Stay honest

Honesty is one of the most underrated virtues of human existence. It is amazing the number of people who take honesty for granted, at least until that moment when they come to realize that there is nothing more important than being honest.

It is not just about being honest with others, but the most important person you have to be honest with is yourself. You cannot keep lying to yourself every other time that you will change and do nothing in the long run.

Adapt, Improvise and Overcome. If you continue to use the same tactics, whether it be in selling, playing football or fighting on the battlefield, soon your enemies or competition will know your plays and be able to outwit you. Each day you have to look at how you are going about things, make the required changes and you will be successful. Thomas Edison once said,

"The definition of insanity is doing the same thing over and over again and expecting different results."

Pressure Reveals Preparation

"When you're under pressure, you don't rise to the occasion, you sink to the level of your training".

Our best strategies and best intentions can quickly go out the window when the bullets start to fly. Don't expect that you or your team will simply rise to the occasion when chaos takes place. Instead, you should have put in enough preparation ahead of time that your worst performance is enough to meet the call of duty. Uncertainty is certain. Surprises are inevitable, and it is your level of discipline and preparation that will determine success or failure. A well prepared individual can meet challenges head-on even when they are caught off balance.

When fighting a 5 round fight you want to have prepared like it was going to be a 10 round war. The preparation needs to have been done in advance so that there is nothing holding you back when the time comes to perform. While your path to success might not require a certain level of physical fitness, it is certainly going to demand preparation in some form. The separation is in the preparation. Be prepared.

Take Responsibility

Be accountable for your actions and admit when you are wrong. SEALs take full responsibility for themselves and their teams. They don't whine and they do not blame others. They win or fail all under their own merit.

Be a Team Player

Don't make it about you. Leave your personal agenda and your personal comfort out of it. Team work is engrained in SEALs right from the get go. They learn that taking care of their team is priority one. They constantly ask themselves how they can make the situation easier or better for each other.

Keep Learning

The devil is in the details. You never know when one little-known fact or detail might make all the difference in the world. There is no end to the education of a US Navy SEAL. Learning is eternal, whether it be in training or simply learning from your mistakes. Having the right mindset around continual learning is paramount for everyone.

Chapter 5: Set Goals Like a Courageous Warrior

Setting goals in life, allows you to move from one point in life to the other, complete with achievements. When you set goals, you can tell whether you have been a success or a failure, based on your ability to accomplish the same.

This is perhaps the most life-changing thing that you will ever get to do for yourself. Not only are you in a good position to work hard at meeting and beating these goals, but they also set the tone for further accomplishments in the future.

You should think and see through your goals like an unstoppable warrior. Warriors go out with one thing in mind, to win. Nothing short of that target is acceptable, and this is why if they fail, they often come back, think up a new strategy and then head back to it again.

You need to take the same angle when setting your goals. These goals are not supposed to be placeholders, they are supposed to be targets, which have to be met. Ensure your goals are realistic, so that you can set real targets for your life. These three points should guide you on how to set goals appropriately:

- Come up with the bigger picture of what you want to achieve
- Break the end goal into smaller milestones
- Start working on the milestones

Once you are able to do this, you will be on your way to success, having taken the first and really important steps in that direction.

One step at a time

Get the simple things right. Start with your housekeeping. Leave every space you come across better than you found it, especially your own space like your room or you home. Keep it clean and impeccable. Do the same with your personal hygiene and your clothing. Put 100% into these little things and it will pay off in the big picture. You will never succeed with the big goals if you never master the little ones.

Be willing to fail

While on route to your goals and dreams there will come many times when statistically, the odds will not be in your favor. If you don't try, you may be one of those chaps who says, "I was thinking about trying that." You will have sat by and played small yet once again. You simply can't look at life through a lens of fear. If you take a calculated risk and fail, at the very least you have a valuable learning experience. Failure is part of the forward movement process. There can be no success without failure. Pick yourself up. And never, ever, be out of the fight.

Importance of Imagery

The mind is a rather interesting part of the human body. You can teach it to think and see what you need it to see. It is all about neuroplasticity. The mind can be coached into appreciating what you need it to appreciate, and this is where imagery comes in handy. Think about yourself finally succeeding in life, achieving your goals. Alongside the success you have achieved, think about the skills that you will need to get there. With these taken into consideration, you will then need to keep this at the back of your mind, and the longer you think about it, the more it begins to play out. Watch it like a motion picture in your mind.

Never underestimate the need for smaller goals in life. It is upon these that you are able to build on and work harder. Short term goals are a very good way of inspiring yourself to do better. This is because you will be accomplishing them every once in a while, on a frequent basis. The frequency of these small victories will get you accustomed to the niceties that come with them, and with time your mind will accept the need to keep achieving these short term goals.

Remember, Rome never came to be in one day, so infers the saying, but it took time, lots of time, years even, for the great Roman Empire to be the legend whose tales have lived on for years, and more to come.

When you set on this course, there is no turning back; there is no falling back either. You hit the start button and it's full speed ahead. Maintain and build on more momentum, soldier on and build on your confidence, and you will be happier in the long run.

The HIT List

You need to come up with an action list, a plan or a course of action. Just wishing or dreaming about the future will not get you what you need. You must be bold enough to soldier on and work on getting closer to the end result.

There are a number of things that you have to do to come up with such a plan. However, for the plan to work in the first place, you need to have a clear vision, and a purpose to go over these goals.

The following are some simple steps that will help you work around this:

- Determine what you need to do

- Be realistic and specific in the plans you make

- Come up with realistic milestones

- Set timelines on everything you are working on

- Mark deliverables off your list when you achieve them

These are things that you are supposed to do on a daily basis. Your plan will only work if you are determined every other day you wake. You need to spur yourself, challenge yourself every morning. Go to sleep with a plan for the day ahead, wake up with a burning desire to beat those plans.

Going through life without goals is not something that we need to be discussing in this age and time. Action, your life should be about action. With action comes impact, and with impact, you effect change. Make the change in your life today, no one can do it better than you can.

Chapter 6: Hone In On The Target

Honing in on the target, is all about putting an emphasis on what you want to achieve. You might have already set it in your mind, done everything possible to clear your schedule of obstacles. It is now time to do what it takes to get there.

It is more like going out to rescue someone from a danger zone. Before you get to the place where the hostage is being kept, you will have to fend off enemy fire from all angles. You have to weed out the distractions. Take them out one by one, break down the enemy's defense line, until you have none but the people or the security system that is keeping you from the hostage. Once you get to this point, it is like making the final home run to win. You know you have to bring home the hostage, alive and unharmed if possible.

This requires a heightened level of focus. Having gone through all the trouble to get here, it would be a pity for you to make one simple mistake and loose it all. Remember when we discussed meditation and how important it is? Well, surely it now comes in handy, right?

Narrow your focus

Narrow your focus to one major thing, define it well and then focus with intensity until you make it happen. Ask yourself, "Do tasks I have planned get me closer to achieving my main objective?"

The important thing about focus is that you eliminate all other possibilities and the risk of making creating errors.

SEALs manage their focus by expending their mental energy wisely. They practice 4 x 4 breathing techniques by inhaling deeply for 4 seconds and follow with four seconds of steady exhaling. They will do this for at least one minute to control stress and arousal. Calm down and focus.

Never Be Late

Being late is a difficult habit for most to break. Being chronically late creates a self-sustaining negative loop that amplifies anxiety and frustration. This behavior can be changed. Most of us have the intention of arriving on time. The problem with this is that life always gets in the way. There are too many variables that can throw this kind of timing out the window in a single moment. The only way to truly be on time is to arrive early. Give yourself some buffer time to absorb any of life's curveballs.

If you're early, you're on time. If you're on time, you're late.

Time management

Optimize your time and your day like a US NAVY SEAL. You need to optimize every single hour in your day, and use it to deliver top notch results. SEALs execute on precision based timing. One minute too early or one minute too late is the difference between life and death.

There are many traps and pitfalls in a day that will devour your precious time. You need to protect it and organize it in such a way that it is rarely ever wasted.

Tasks can always be completed quicker than you might have thought. If something usually takes you 5 minutes to complete, then try pushing yourself to finish it in 4 minutes. You will be surprised at what you find.

You are going to need all the extra time that you can conjure up to work on your new path.

Thrive in a network

Not so many people, in fact very few people at all are able to understand what makes a US Navy Seal. Most of us normal creatures are not able to fathom what they go through, or reason like they do. With this in mind therefore, it is always easier for them to thrive in their own groups.

Similarly, you will need to find likeminded individuals who share in the same perspective as you do, to inspire you to do better. It is about empowering one another. At this juncture, someone like your mentor or your life coach will definitely come in handy.

The most important thing about being in a network of good friends, is the fact that you are able to discuss your goals, challenges in life or on your path to whichever target you have set your mind on, and you might even share useful tips that will help you get there faster and better than you would ever have thought.

~ A problem shared is a problem solved~

Chapter 7: Train Like an Elite Warrior

It is one thing to want to do something, and it is a whole different concept to follow through with it. Seals understand only one thing; to do. They do not try, they do not make attempts. Navy Seals simply go out, execute a plan and get results.

You too can execute and get results, and it starts with training yourself to become the elite person you want to become. The following are some simple routines that will help you get that discipline you need in order to be the perfect example of you. Remember, the only obstacle you will ever encounter in your life, bigger than any other you might ever come across, is yourself.

Develop an exercise routine that pushes you mentally as well as physically

Extremely vigorous exercise can be quite painful and uncomfortable. SEALs use this type of exercise to push their discomfort thresholds to the limit without injuring their bodies. The more they can endure in practice the more successful they will be in the field. They retrain their minds to accept difficulty and even welcome it.

There are so many exercise routines that you can work around. All of these are designed specifically to deliver one thing or the other.

Towards this end, try and get yourself into an exercise routine, one where you will not only benefit physically, but a routine that will push you to the limits mentally. I recommend doing this in a team environment as SEALs do to keep you motivated and engaged.

Sweating it out

Is sweating healthy? This is a very common question that most people would like to find an answer to. The main reason why people try to find an answer to this question is mainly because a good number tend to either sweat too much, while there are also a few who sweat a little less than they would consider normal. In such a scenario therefore it makes a lot of sense for you to wonder whether sweating is actually normal or not, and besides that whether sweating is actually healthy.

In as far as the issue of healthiness is concerned it is important to note that sweating is actually healthy. It is one of the means through which the body actually excretes some impurities. As a matter of fact there are so many important uses of sweating that should be noted. Let us consider some of them herein

Sweating is important to the body in a number of ways, which include but are not necessarily limited to the following:-

- Cleansing the body
- Controlling the body temperature

With that in mind the amount of sweat that someone exudes from their body can mean a lot. When you come to think of it, it is important to mention that excessive sweating is actually a medical condition that requires immediate attention. Medically those who sweat a lot are usually said to be undergoing something known as hyperhidrosis. In such a case, someone actually sweats more that the average person does. In fact those who undergo this kind of condition usually sweat even when the weather is cold, or when the temperatures are cooler.

For a number of those who are affected by this condition, the sweating usually occurs in the palms or even the sole of their feet, while a common occurrence is in the underarms. Thus in the event that you find yourself in such a situation, you need to really consider seeking medical assistance before things get out of hand.

Excessive sweating (hyperhidrosis) is a condition that is suffered by so many people in the world today, and a recent statistic puts that figure to millions of people worldwide. This means that like other common ailments like the common flu, it is prevalent. Besides that, there are so many people who undergo this condition and assume that their bodies have simply gone into overdrive.

One of the things that is worth mentioning about the condition is that the root cause is yet to be convincingly determined, though there are several reports that have been advocated so far. Anxiety is one of the common reasons why people sweat too much, though this is usually in localized situations in most cases. Apart from anxiety, overstimulation of the nerves responsible for the action of the sweat glands is also a cause of excessive sweating, or even response to stimuli by the sweat glands. In such a scenario, the sweat glands are probably very sensitive to the stimuli, whether internal or external.

It is thus important to mention that sweating however important to the bodily functions can be a damning experience in the event that you sweat too much. Hence should you experience this, it is important that you see a medical officer as soon as you can.

Push your body to prepare your mind

If you only see the nature of SEAL training as overly rigorous and physical then you are missing the big picture. These elite warriors are training their minds. The intense physicality of their training is a byproduct of consistent mental conditioning. They learn the valuable lesson of getting comfortable in the uncomfortable.

Everything that you do in life is all about what happens in your mind. Your body simply relays the instructions that it receives from upstairs. With this in mind therefore, it is important for you to try and make sure that you do some exercises which will push your mind to the limits.

The human brain can be trained to learn anything you put your mind to. You have to push your body in order for your mind to feel comfortable in the worst situations.

Exercise and Feel better about yourself

Exercise improves our mood, controls weight gain, promotes better sleep and boosts our energy levels. In general, exercise will make you feel better about yourself. Create a minimum 30 minute aerobic exercise routine daily.

Your mind will love what you are doing, and the impetus to keep working hard will be innate.

Diet + Healthy food = Healthy mind

Are you on a diet? Have you ever thought about being on a diet? Well, here's something that you need to know, dieting is good for your body, and your mind. There are diets out there, fad diets, which do not yield results, or if they do, you will be more frustrated throughout, which negates the entire principle that we are trying to work on.

Make sure you are eating a healthy diet. It is very good for your body, very good for your mind, and most importantly, very good for the cause that we are trying to achieve.

Whenever we mention diets, some people take things overboard, and start fasting – this is not dieting, that is torture! Just try to eat healthy food, drink lots of water, have vegetables and fruits regularly and you will be good to go.

There are so many different kinds of diet plans in the world today that you can consider working around especially if you are looking to get some really good results in the process. There are so many people who are on diets today, and the one thing that most of them are keen on is weight loss or trying to maintain a particular body shape, or body mass. There are several diets that are available for several purposes. However, it is important to take note of some of the common things that these diets share. One thing that you must always remember is that most of these diets can be basic diet programs, but when you take them seriously, you will realize that there is so much more to them than meets the eye. As a matter of fact, a lot of these diets are life changers if you take them seriously, and your life will most certainly benefit from them.

There are several diet programs that you need to take note of. These include the following:

The Pritikin Diet – this diet is usually advisable for those who are looking to reverse or take preventive measures against heart disease, and as a result it is considered closely vegetarian. The diet focuses on daily exercise, high fiber foods, fruits, vegetables and low cholesterol food.

The Macrobiotic diet – this is another vegetarian diet program that seeks to promote overall health and has been claimed to help in curing diseases like cancer, though there is no proof to this end yet. The foundation of this diet lies in the use of brown rice and whole grains.

In terms of dieting, you have to make sure that your body is well hydrated. Because of this you have to drink a lot of water or the recommended amount of water on a daily basis so that you are able to get your system refreshed. If you are taking coffee, make sure that it is de-caffeinated by all means. This is good for you. Besides that it is also important for you to take vitamin supplements. These vitamin supplements are also supposed to include some minerals that are good enough for your body.

Never forget to exercise on a daily basis. Exercise is good for you since it keeps you active and keeps your body systems in a good functioning state. In terms of the exercise, remember that you only need to take it step by step. You can go to the gym, but do not act like you are trying to bring the gold medal home; just be easy and you will get it right.

Never forget to eat, and eat well. Being on a diet does not mean that you are not supposed to eat. Make sure that you can eat properly, and also make sure that you do not get to overeat. You should only eat to satisfy your appetite.

Generally diets are supposed to make you feel much better about yourself as a whole. This therefore means that you need to make sure that you are able to get the best out of whichever diet you are practicing. However, it is important for you to take note of the limits of the diet and your personal limits. This is important so that you do not get to push yourself overboard.

CHAPTER 8: MEDITATE LIKE A SEAL

SEALs use sacred silence to tap into the deeper parts of their minds. If a SEAL is in a submarine or a snipers nest for an extended period of time they will need to remain calm and focused.

Whenever you talk about meditation, a lot of people simply think about the yogis and find it to be a rather amusing spectacle altogether. For a long time, the benefits of meditation are things that have commonly remained known only to those who have been keen on doing the same. However, we have to debunk some of these benefits, share them with you too, so that you know for sure what you are missing out on, and why it is important for you to partake in the same.

One of the core elements of meditation is silence. It is the deathly silence that can make you think there is no one around, yet you are truly in the presence of a lot of people, hundreds if not thousands perhaps. It is the kind of silence that makes you think and see things clearly, see things from a whole new perspective.

Tap into deeper sections of your mind

Remember when we started this earlier on, we emphasized on how important it is for you to train your mind to do things differently? How important it is to show your mind that the status quo, is just a situation, nothing more nothing less. Well, when we come to the meditation square, there is more truth to this than you would ever have imagined.

Ideally, meditation is all about tapping into the deepest part of your mind, to find clarity. You will be able to get clarity through this, much better than you have ever managed to do so through any other means.

If you can sit in a room or in a space with people for such a long time, quiet and devoid of any distractions at all, you can rest assured that there is nothing that you will ever have to worry about with respect to meditation.

But why is meditation important, you might ask yourself?

Through meditation, you are able to learn and appreciate the importance of being quiet and getting a new perspective into life. The benefits of meditation have been studied by scientists in coordination with the Dalai Lama and Buddhists monks. What was found was that the brains of people who meditated often actually had more activity in the positive centers of the brain. Moreover, those who have been through depression or anxiety can actually reroute their brain's set points, allowing them to be more open to positivity and more closed to negativity.

While loss and difficult situations are impossible to ignore or stop, there is a choice as to how to react to those negative emotions. It is the brain's response, then, that allows certain people to brush off negativity while others can't. This is not to say that depression is a choice because it most certainly isn't. No one would choose depression when other options are available. It simply means that even a depressed mind can reduce those feelings of depression by taking the time to meditate and relax the system. When the brain gets a pause in the constant barrage of thoughts, ideas, and problems, it is allowed to make more positive connections in the neurons.

The body can heal itself if it is given the proper tools. In many cases, all the body needs is to be cleared of harmful substances in order to be free to work properly. This includes the workings of the mind. If the mind is directed toward positivity and healing, the body will be more likely to heal itself. One major reason people get sick is due to stress breaking down the body's natural ability to function, so meditation can be used to help reduce stress on the mind, consequently freeing the mind and body for positive energy.

In scientific terms, meditation has actually been proven to decrease cortisol, which is the hormone associated with stress. Meditation also reduced the heart rate, respiration, and metabolic rate. When meditating, activity in the prefrontal cortex is increased, and the immune system is better supported. This is all on top of the benefit of a feeling of relaxation. Because of these consequences, meditation can reduce stress related to work or other stressors. It can also help lessen feelings of anxiety and depression, improve cognitive function, and improve immunities.

Daily meditations can have a huge impact on quality of life. All of these benefits are free, just by allowing the mind to be in a state of meditation at some point during the day. Some people do this as soon as they awake or right before bed. Other good times might be on a lunch break or while any children in the home are napping or at school. Any quiet time is good, as long as it is done.

Benefits of meditation

There are so many things that you stand to gain when you meditate. Your body and your physique in general will appreciate this exercise. The following are some of the true benefits that you will enjoy when you are meditating:

- Reduced anxiety
- Improved management of panic attacks

- Reduce the concentration of grey matter on your brain
- Decrease the need for sleep, by improving your psychomotor vigilance
- Improve and enhance your attention and focus, and your ability to work under stressful conditions
- Heightened level of decision making and information processing
- Helps you achieve better resilience, mental strength and emotional intelligence
- You survive more pain, but feel less of it than before
- It is a better pain reliever than morphine
- Helps you be more aware of yourself, and your surroundings

Conclusion

Earn Your Trident Everyday

The Navy SEAL's Trident is an amazing looking emblem that only few men will ever have the honor to wear. It has an eagle clutching an anchor, a trident, and a flintlock pistol. It represents freedom (eagle), the Navy (anchor), the mythological character Poseidon (whose scepter was the trident). He was King of the Ocean, where the SEALs feel most at home. Lastly, the pistol represents a SEAL's capability on land. It is always cocked and ready to fire, which symbolizes a SEAL's need to be ready at all times.

The statement *Earn Your Trident Every Day* is a reminder to continue to hold your standards high and never slip back into the person you once were. It is a reminder to live with purpose, honor and integrity. It is a reminder to do what is right every day. It is a reminder that hard work is never finished and that you must forge on with your learning and growing every single day.

Life is full of challenges, which have to be overcome every day. There are times when you will feel so energized and determined that the obstacles in your path will simply obliterate right before your eyes. There will also be those times when you will feel like you are in the basement and you want to quit. During these times remember to read the SEAL Code out loud and pick yourself back up.

There is a common saying that if you stay ahead in first position for so long, you might never know when the game has changed behind you. This is so true. Many are the times when we have seen in sporting activities, teams that lead for a very long time normally have a difficult time getting back to the helm when they get toppled. This is because it takes them a longer time to adapt first to the situation, and secondly to the realization that they were not as superior as they would have thought they were in the first place. Remember to be adaptable.

As you pursue your own goals and dreams, remember to keep the model of the SEALs in mind. This book has created an outline for you to follow in terms of the processes and traits required to become the self-motivated person that you desire to be. No longer will you be someone who sits on the sidelines only dreaming of achieving your goals. Now, you will be the person who works hard to realize them, and is then able to enjoy the satisfaction of having taken yourself to a new place in life. SEALs are well respected not because of their physical capabilities, but rather because of the mental strength that they demonstrate under some of the most difficult conditions imaginable.

You are capable of great things in life. As long as you believe that to be true, the sky is the limit. Remember, no one is born a Navy SEAL.

The pathway to motivation and success is defined by many things. You need to increase your confidence by taking action. You must find passion and persevere for long-term goals. Embrace an elite warrior mindset and work towards personal development every day.

Good Luck!

THE SEAL CODE

- Loyalty to Country, Team and Teammate
- Serve with Honor and Integrity On and Off the Battlefield
- Ready to Lead, Ready to Follow, Never Quit
- Take responsibility for your actions and the actions of your teammates
- Excel as Warriors through Discipline and Innovation
- Train for War, Fight to Win, Defeat our Nation's Enemies
- Earn your Trident everyday

Made in the USA
San Bernardino, CA
14 February 2017